W9-ABM-008

WITHDRAWN

Great Minds of Science

AR 7.2/3.0

Edward Jenner

Conqueror of Smallpox

Ana María Rodríguez, 1958-

Enslow Publishers, Inc.

40 Industrial Road   PO Box 38
Box 398   Aldershot
Berkeley Heights, NJ 07922   Hants GU12 6BP
USA   UK

http://www.enslow.com

Library of Congress Cataloging-in-Publication Data

Rodriguez, Ana Maria, 1958-
   Edward Jenner : conqueror of smallpox / Ana Maria Rodriguez.
     p. cm. — (Great minds of science)
   Includes bibliographical references and index.
   ISBN-10: 0-7660-2504-7
   1. Jenner, Edward, 1749-1823—Juvenile literature. 2. Physicians—
England—Biography—Juvenile literature. 3. Smallpox—Vaccination—
History—Juvenile literature. I. Title. II. Series.
   R489.J5R63 2006
   614.5'21'092—dc22

                              2005019088

   ISBN-13: 978-0-7660-2504-2

Printed in the United States of America

10 9 8 7 6 5 4 3

To Our Readers:
We have done our best to make sure all Internet addresses in this book were
active and appropriate when we went to press. However, the author and the
publisher have no control over and assume no liability for the material
available on those Internet sites or on other Web sites they may link to. Any
comments or suggestions can be sent by e-mail to comments@enslow.com or
to the address on the back cover.

Illustration Credits: Bettmann/CORBIS, p. 80; Blocker History of
Medicine Collections, UTMB, pp. 17, 41, 68, 70, 75, 93; Enslow
Publishers, Inc., p. 24; F. A. Murphy and S. Whitfield/CDC, 1975,
p. 13; G. Bernard/Photo Researchers, p. 53; G. McCarthy/CORBIS,
p. 44; National Library of Medicine, pp. 30, 33, 49, 88, 95;
R. Tidman/CORBIS, p. 59; World Health Organization (W.H.O.),
pp. 10, 104; World Health Organization (W.H.O.)/J. Wickett, p. 108.

Cover Illustration: Blocker History of Medicine Collections, UTMB
(foreground); F. A. Murphy and S. Whitfield/CDC, 1975 (background).

Contents

1
"A Terrifying Experience"

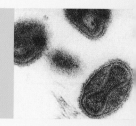

EIGHT-YEAR-OLD EDWARD JENNER entered the old stables with apprehension. He was not alone. A few other children went in with him. They were not going to play a game or explore the dark corners of the stables. They were going to experience what probably was the most terrifying ordeal of their lives.

Edward and his companions were going to be inoculated. They were going to be infected on purpose with a mild form of the most dangerous disease of the time. This disease was smallpox.

In 1757 there was a smallpox epidemic in Edward's town. Smallpox was spreading rapidly in the area around Berkeley, a town in England. It was affecting many people at the same time.

The doctors had strongly recommended inoculating the children who had never had the disease. Inoculation was the only way to protect them from catching a deadly form of smallpox. And they were right. In Edward's time smallpox was a very common fatal disease. It killed up to one of every three people infected. Most of the victims were children.

To protect Edward and the other children from smallpox, their families had arranged for the local apothecary, or pharmacist, to provide the inoculations. The apothecary was Mr. Holbrow. Mr. Holbrow could not go to the children's homes to inoculate them. Neither could he do it at his home or at a hospital. Edward and his friends had to be inoculated in a place where they would not be in contact with any other person. After the inoculation they would have to remain quarantined, or isolated, for a few weeks. They had to be quarantined to prevent passing on smallpox to other people. Mr. Holbrow did the inoculations in his stables.[1]

Inoculation in the 18th Century

Inoculation was a rapid procedure. They called it the "arm-to-arm transfer." Mr. Holbrow took Edward's arm and made a small cut with a sharp instrument called a lancet. It looked like a small knife. Then, he placed a small amount of the pus from a blister of a smallpox victim in the cut. Finally, Mr. Holbrow wrapped the cut with a clean bandage.

Edward and his friends did not leave the stables until they were cured of the mild case of smallpox. They ate, slept, and stayed all day and night in the poorly ventilated stables, surrounded by a terrible stench.

Inoculation itself might have felt to Edward like nothing when compared with the preparations for inoculation he went through. The doctors believed then that to increase the chances of a successful inoculation, the patients had to be "prepared" for it. Doctors prepared their patients by providing them with a very light diet and medicines that would purge, or empty, their bowels. They also bled them often.

The doctors prepared their patients this way because they believed purging, bleeding, and a light diet would clean the inside of their bodies. A clean body, they thought, would have a better chance for a successful inoculation. Today doctors know that these preparations did not help the body. On the contrary, they weakened it and caused a lot of unnecessary suffering.

This is how Edward described years later the preparation he went through. For six weeks "there was taking of blood until the blood was thin; purging until the body was wasted to a skeleton; and starving on a vegetable diet to keep it so."[2]

Edward and his friends survived their inoculations. Edward came out of the stables extremely weak. He needed to rest for a month to recuperate. He never forgot this deeply traumatic experience. It was obvious to him that there had to be a better way to prevent smallpox. Little did he know at that moment that he would be the one to discover the first safe way to prevent the most deadly disease in human history.

The History of Smallpox

Smallpox, even in its mild form, was one of the worst scourges, or causes of suffering, people had ever experienced. People also called it by the name of variola. This word comes from the Latin word *varius*, which means "spotted." Sometimes they called it the "red death" or the "speckled monster" because it turned people's skin red and speckled.[3]

The cause of smallpox is a type of germ called a virus. The virus is in the droplets people breathe or cough out. People get infected when they breathe in airborne viruses. In the case of smallpox, the virus was also in the pus and other body fluids. Touching people with smallpox or their pus-stained clothing could also infect people.

Scientists are not sure when the first case of smallpox appeared. The oldest evidence seems to be from about 1500 B.C. The evidence comes from the mummy of the Egyptian pharaoh Ramses V. The mummy shows the typical marks of a smallpox infection. There is a rash of pimples over the face and hands of the pharaoh's mummy.[4]

The Pharaoh's Plight

Ramses V might have been a powerful ruler of Egypt, but this did not save him from becoming infected with smallpox, just as his subjects did. In two to three weeks, smallpox decided the fate of Ramses V. The first symptoms, or indications, that Ramses V had caught smallpox were violent shivers and high fever. He also might have felt sharp pain, especially in his lower back. These symptoms went away in one or two days.

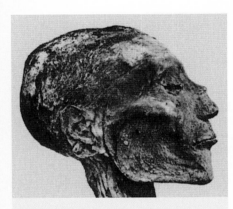

Even Pharaohs could not escape the scourge of smallpox. The mummified head of Ramses V, above, shows pockmarks on his cheeks, signifying smallpox.

After the fever and pain had passed, red spots appeared on the pharaoh's face. Then, more spots appeared on his neck and shoulders. Finally, they covered all his body. In a couple of days the spots became blisters filled with a yellow liquid called pus. The blisters burst open, releasing the pus. Ramses V had a fever again. He also dreaded drinking or eating. More blisters covered his tongue and throat, making swallowing very painful.

Ramses V's caregivers must have felt a lot of pity for him at this point. His skin was red and swollen, burning with fever. He could barely keep his eyes open because of the swelling. Some of his opened blisters might have bled. He was in pain, and his body smelled like rotten flesh.[5]

It seems that Ramses V died of smallpox. If he had survived, about ten days after the disease started, the open blisters would have dried and formed scabs. Around ten days later, the scabs would have fallen off. However, his skin would have been marked with pits.

Learning Lessons

The doctors of powerful Ramses V could do nothing to ease his suffering. Over three thousand years ago, there was nothing doctors could do to cure smallpox. The same is true even today. However, there were two very important facts people knew. First, smallpox did not develop the same way in everybody. Some people had a "minor," or mild case with a few pimples from which they recovered without problems. Others had a "major," or severe, case of smallpox with numerous pimples that bled.

The patients with variola major had a lower chance of survival than those with variola minor. The "major" form killed as many as one in every three people infected. On the other hand, the "minor" form was less deadly. It killed about one of every ten people infected.

The second fact about smallpox was that people who survived either form of the disease would never get sick with it again. They would be "immune to," or protected against, a second smallpox attack. These solid facts made people come up with the idea of inoculations to protect children from deadly variola major. Why not avoid the most deadly form of smallpox by "protecting" children with a minor form of the disease?

The first inoculations seem to have begun in

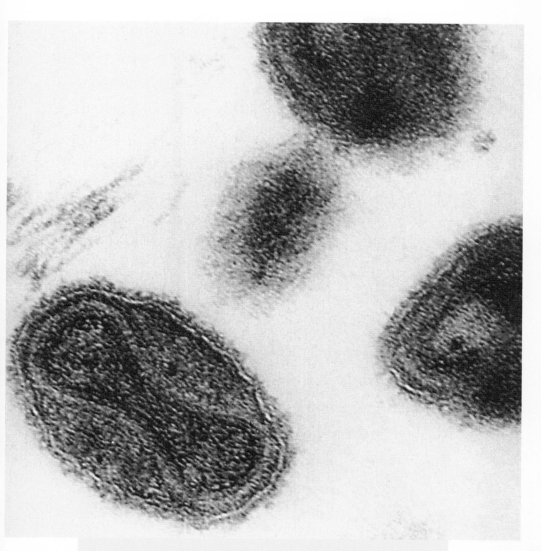

The smallpox virus enlarged about 370,000 times using Transmission Electron Microscopy. The dumbbell-shaped structure inside the virion is the viral core, which contains the viral DNA.

China at the end of the seventeenth century. Around 1721 Lady Mary Wortley Montagu, who was a smallpox survivor, introduced smallpox inoculations in England after she had learned about them in Turkey. In Wales during the 1800s, people called inoculations "buying the smallpox."[6]

Inoculations were the best weapon people had to fight smallpox. Yet people could still die from an inoculation. They could still pass the disease on to other people.

When Edward Jenner grew up, he became a doctor. Every time Edward assisted his tutor in giving inoculations, he remembered vividly how traumatic the experience was for him. One of the patients was a young milkmaid. She claimed she did not need to be inoculated. She said she was already protected from smallpox because she had had the cowpox. Jenner listened carefully. Cowpox was a disease of cows. It could affect people too, but very mildly. Was it possible to protect people from deadly smallpox by infecting them with a mild cow disease?[7]

2

Rough Beginnings

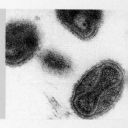

EDWARD JENNER WAS BORN INTO A BIG family. Before his birth on May 17, 1749, seven brothers and sisters had already been born in the Jenners' home. But these were rough times for children living in England, and all over the world. Before Edward was born, two of his brothers had died while they were still young children.

During Edward's time, as many as one in every three children in rural England died. One of the main reasons for this high mortality was famine, or the lack of enough food. Other reasons were diseases such as smallpox and typhoid fever.

Back then people did not know that germs cause diseases. For this reason, they did not find it necessary to wash their hands and bodies often. They did not know that having a clean body and a clean house would help them stay healthy. Many children living in the seventeen and eighteen hundreds, like Edward's brothers, died of diseases that would not be serious health problems today.

Edward had three living sisters and two living brothers when he was born. He was the youngest member of the family. The oldest was nineteen-year-old Mary, followed by seventeen-year-old Stephen. Then came thirteen-year-old Henry and eleven-year-old Sarah. Annie was just eight years old when Edward joined the family.

Since it was common for some of the children in a family to die, many parents would name a new baby after a brother or sister who had passed away. This was the case with Edward Jenner. He received the name of his five-year-old brother, who had died two weeks before he was born.

Jenner's Parents

Edward's father, Stephen Jenner, was an educated man. He had studied at Pembroke

Jenner's nephew described him as shorter than average, with dark, curly hair. He was nearsighted, but never used glasses. He usually dressed in black, with a large collar to the coat and loose, low trousers, just like other doctors of the time. Note the dairymaid and cows in the background.

College in Oxford and became a clergyman. As a clergyman, Stephen had his own church and conducted religious services for the Berkeley community. Around 1729 Stephen Jenner became the vicar, or priest, of the parish church of Berkeley.

In the same year Stephen married Sarah Head. She was the daughter of Reverend Henry Head, the vicar Stephen had replaced in Berkeley. Stephen moved into the vicarage, or the house of the vicar, in Berkeley, and began his new life with his wife, Sarah. The Jenners lived comfortably with the salary the church paid Reverend Jenner for his services to the community. The Jenner family also received income from the lease of their own land and other property. Mrs. Jenner took care of the household chores and the children's well-being and basic education.

Growing Up

The family home seemed to have been a good place for the Jenner children to grow up. The children must have played in and explored the gardens planted with tall trees, green bushes, and flowers, such as golden yellow marigolds and small bright blue forget-me-nots.[1]

The Jenners probably went fishing in the pond and learned to ride the horses that lived in the stables surrounding their home. Horseback riding was an essential skill to learn in Edward's time. During the seventeen and eighteen hundreds in rural England, the horse was the main means of transportation, along with horse-pulled carriages.

When Edward was born, Berkeley had about two thousand people living in as many as five hundred houses. Edward wrote once that Berkeley "has the name of a town, but in size it is a mere village."[2] The town rests on the side of a hill. From there people can see immense green pastures, the forest of Dene, and the calm river Severn that make up the Valley of Severn.

Berkeley was mainly a farming community. People grew many grass crops, including hay for the cattle and grass for the sheep. They produced a variety of dairy products such as butter and rich double Gloucester cheese that is still produced today. They sold these products in the markets of the nearby towns of Bristol and Bath.

Edward lived in this small and quiet farming community most of his life. The only exceptions were the two years he spent in London studying medicine and brief visits he made later in his life. Edward was strongly attached to Berkeley and its people. He never wanted to live anywhere else.

Edward's brothers, Stephen and Henry, followed in their father's footsteps. They went to college and became clergymen. They were at Oxford when Edward was between one and four years old. So Edward probably played mostly with his three sisters.

Edward's mother and sisters cared for him while they attended the holiday services celebrated at his father's church, the Berkeley market day on Wednesdays, and social family gatherings at the Berkeley vicarage. Sadly, a tragic family loss shattered this peaceful existence when Edward was five years old.

In October 1754 Mrs. Jenner gave birth to her ninth child, Thomas. But Thomas was not a healthy baby. He was baptized at the Berkeley church on October 8 and buried on the ninth. Mrs. Jenner was very ill too, and she died the next day. She was just forty-six years old. The Jenners had not recovered from her tragic loss when, almost exactly two months later, Reverend Jenner passed away on December 9. He was fifty-two.

Edward had lost his mother and his father in just two months. He was now a five-year-old orphan. Fortunately, his oldest sister, Mary, and his aunt, Deborah, took care of him, taking over the role of mother. For the next three years Edward's life seems to have continued in the same way as before the loss of his parents.

After Reverend Jenner died, his oldest son, Stephen, took responsibility for the family. He managed their income and took care of the family property and business. Stephen also played the role of father figure for Edward. He acted like a father to him for the rest of his life.

School Days

Edward attended grammar, or elementary, school. The school was free and located in the long and narrow market town of Wotton-under-Edge. In Edward's time, only boys attended grammar school. Girls did not go to school, as they do today. However, Edward's sisters had learned basic math, music, and how to read and write at home.

Edward boarded, or lived, with the schoolmaster, Reverend Thomas Clissold. Before Edward went to grammar school, his sisters had already taught him how to read and write English. Grammar school was not like elementary school today. The boys studied grammar, but not English grammar. They studied Latin grammar, mostly by memorization. Sometimes they also studied Greek.

Edward was not an outstanding student. He

did not enjoy learning the classical languages, Latin and Greek. He did not enjoy studying French either, which was the language most educated people in Europe spoke at the time. However, he learned enough of these languages to graduate from grammar school and to avoid being whipped by the teachers. He once wrote, "I went through the ordinary course of a classical education [and] obtained a tolerable proficiency in the Latin language, and got a decent smattering of Greek."[3]

For Edward the most important part of his school years was not learning the classics. What left a long-lasting impression on him was observing and studying nature. Edward developed a passion for natural history. He began by collecting the nests of field mice. His collection seems to have contained over fifty nests. He also collected many fossils he found in limestone hills around his home. He always derived more pleasure from long walks in the hills and forests in the valley than from books and formal classes at school.

Edward Jenner: Conqueror of Smallpox

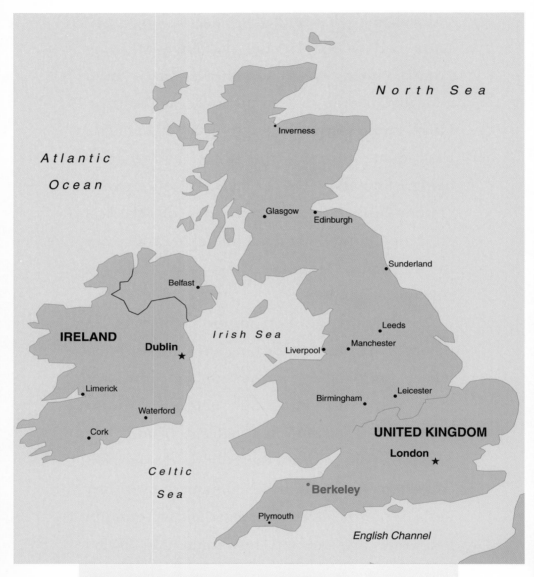

North Sea

Atlantic Ocean

Inverness

Glasgow

Edinburgh

Sunderland

Belfast

IRELAND

Dublin ★

Irish Sea

Leeds

Manchester

Liverpool

Limerick

Waterford

Birmingham

Leicester

Cork

UNITED KINGDOM

London ★

Celtic Sea

Berkeley

Plymouth

English Channel

Edward Jenner lived in England all his life. Outside of his two years in London, Jenner never left Berkeley.

His education in grammar school was interrupted by a most traumatic event. When Edward was eight years old, smallpox struck Berkeley, and his brothers and sisters decided it was best for him to be inoculated.

This experience marked him for life. For a few years after the inoculation, he had to receive constant medical attention to take care of his health. Edward resumed his attendance at grammar school after the inoculation.

Edward graduated from grammar school when he was twelve years old. Then it was time to decide what profession he would enter. It is not clear whether it was Edward or his family who decided on a career in medicine. What is clear from his years in grammar school is that his interests did not rest with the classical languages, which were a basic requirement to become a clergyman like his father and brothers. Edward's passion was the study of natural phenomena. At the time, the career that fitted his interests the best was medicine.

Becoming a Doctor

One of the ways to become a family doctor at that time was to be an apprentice to, or a student of, another doctor. And this is what Edward did. He moved to Chipping Sudbury, a nearby town, and worked with Mr. John Ludlow. With Mr. Ludlow, Edward learned what he had to know to practice as a family doctor.

3

Going to London

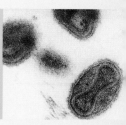

THE YEAR 1770 WAS VERY IMPORTANT TO Edward Jenner. He was twenty-one years old and had learned from Mr. Ludlow all he needed to know to become a country doctor. He could now establish his practice in Berkeley and stay close to his family. However, his nine-year-long apprenticeship had sparked his interest in medicine. Jenner wanted to continue his education in the medical field. He decided to move to London for two years. This would be the first time he would be living far away from his family.

This must have been a difficult decision for Jenner. He was not an adventuresome person. He was not the kind that would "set out into the world to seek his fortune."[1] Nevertheless, Jenner knew that there was much more to learn about medicine in London schools. If he wanted to continue his studies, he needed to find a tutor and a good medical school in London. He found them in the newspaper.

Jenner sent his pupil, or student, application to Dr. John Hunter. Dr. Hunter was one of the best scientific minds of Jenner's time. He became not only Jenner's tutor but also his life-long friend. Dr. Hunter had practiced as an army doctor before moving to London. In London he had a private practice, seeing patients at his home. He also practiced and taught medicine at Saint George's Hospital. Dr. Hunter was also known for his work as a scientist.

John Hunter was one of the scientists living in the eighteenth century who believed in a hands-on approach to the study of nature. There were scientists at that time who tried to understand nature by speculation, using only their imaginations to come up with explanations for natural phenomena. But not Hunter. He believed that "knowledge grew only out of experiment and observation."[2]

Life in London

When Jenner moved to London, he lived in John Hunter's house on Jermyn Street. Jenner was one of Hunter's first pupils. Here, Hunter constantly encouraged Jenner to plan and carry out experiments. Hunter did not want Jenner to use speculation to find out how things work. He always told him, "But why think? Why not try the experiment?"[3]

During the two years Jenner spent in London he took medical courses at Saint George's Hospital, where Hunter gave lectures. He took classes in chemistry, medicine, anatomy (the study of the human body inside and out), and midwifery (the art of helping mothers give birth to their babies). Besides taking courses, Jenner assisted Hunter when he was seeing his patients at home and at the hospital.

A typical day in Jenner's life usually followed his tutor's schedule. The day started early. By

6:00 A.M. Hunter was in the dissecting room working with Jenner. In the dissecting room they dissected, or opened, the dead bodies of animals and people to study the insides in detail.

They ate a light breakfast of toast and tea by 9:00 A.M. After breakfast Hunter saw his patients at home from 10:00 A.M. till noon, and Jenner assisted him. He changed bandages or prepared medications for the patients according to Hunter's instructions.

Precisely at noon, Hunter climbed into his horse-pulled coach and left his home heading for Saint George's Hospital. There he did his rounds, or visited his patients. Jenner accompanied him and assisted him when he had to perform surgery. They finished the hospital rounds at about 2:00 P.M.

John Hunter, or "the dear man" as Jenner called him, was Jenner's tutor, colleague, and friend.

Between 2:00 P.M. and 5:00 P.M., Jenner attended

class. He took notes as he listened to the lectures given by his tutor and other well-known doctors at Saint George's Hospital. Sometimes Jenner took classes at Great Windmill medical school. William Hunter, John's older brother, operated Great Windmill. This school "maintained a reputation for excellence."[4] William Hunter was also a very distinguished and important doctor in England. He was appointed Physician Extraordinaire to the Queen.

After class Jenner hurried back to Hunter's home to have a big dinner. It was probably around 5:00 P.M. However, his daily activities did not end with dessert. After Hunter took an hour nap, they both returned to work in the dissecting room. Sometimes Hunter dictated notes to Jenner about his experiments, and probably the two discussed their latest results. They stayed up till late at night.

It was probably during these evening meetings that Jenner talked to Hunter about cowpox. He told him about what a milkmaid had said in Berkeley, that she claimed she could not "take the smallpox" because she "had the cowpox." Jenner even showed Hunter a drawing of a typical cowpox vesicle, or blister, on the finger of a milkmaid. Hunter listened to Jenner. He did not discourage him from pursuing this study. He probably told him something like, "But why think? Why not try an experiment?"

Jenner enjoyed his life in London as a medical student. He learned a lot about medicine, as he had hoped. However, Jenner did not like living in London. The big city was so different from Berkeley. In the Valley of Severn the air was clean and life was peaceful and quiet. London was the opposite. The streets stank with garbage and dirt, and all kinds of noises plagued the citizens.

Jenner seemed to be particularly annoyed by the black, thick smoke rising from the numerous house chimneys. It did not let him think straight. He once wrote to a friend: "When I write in London, my brain seems full of smoke [which] is too apt to cloud our best faculties."[5]

In spite of not feeling quite at home, Jenner

made the best of his years in London. Besides adding to his medical education, he also made new friends. Some of these friends, like Joseph Banks, helped him later in his career.

In 1771, Banks had returned to London from a three-year-long expedition, a voyage, around the world on the ship *Endeavor*. Banks was the chief botanist and had collected many plants and other specimens never seen in England before. Banks needed somebody to prepare the

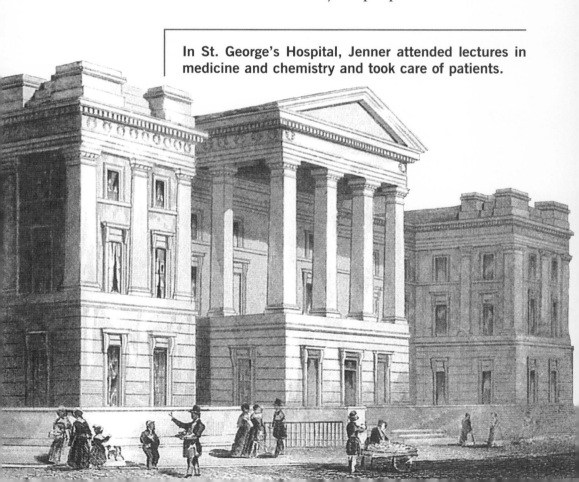

In St. George's Hospital, Jenner attended lectures in medicine and chemistry and took care of patients.

specimens for preservation and to classify them in a catalog.

Banks knew Hunter because they had met at the Royal Society, the most prestigious scientific society of the time. Banks asked Hunter whom he would recommend to take care of the thousands of new specimens he had brought from around he world. Hunter recommended Jenner for the job. He had much experience dissecting animals and plants, and was very good at it.

An Opportunity

Jenner seems to have done a very good job. Banks was so pleased that he invited Jenner to join him on his next expedition around the world, this time on the ship called *Resolution*. This was a good opportunity for Jenner to further his career. He would have the chance to visit unexplored lands and collect animals and plants nobody else in England had seen before. He would become famous, and everybody would respect him and admire him.

But this offer did not appeal to Jenner at all. It did not appeal to him because he was not interested in adventures in faraway lands. During his time living in London Jenner had missed his brother Stephen and his hometown. He just wanted to go back home after he finished his studies. Jenner told a friend that he had refused Banks's offer, "partly guided by the deep and grateful affection . . . for his eldest brother . . . and partly by an attachment to the rural scenes and habits of his early youth."[6]

It would be in the small rural town of Berkeley that Edward Jenner would make one of the greatest contributions to medicine of the eighteenth century.

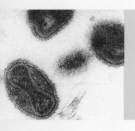

Sleeping Hedgehogs and Burning Candles

EDWARD JENNER MUST HAVE FELT VERY happy to return to his hometown after living in London for two years. He left behind the loud noises, the reeking streets, and the air tainted with the black smoke that bothered him so much.

That Berkeley is where he wanted to be more than anywhere else is clear from his responses to job offers outside Berkeley. In 1771 Jenner had declined Sir Joseph Banks's offer to join an expedition around the world on board the ship *Resolution*. In 1775 John Hunter asked him to join him as a doctor, teacher, and scientist in London. This offer would have opened the doors to a fine clientele and a very profitable practice. Again Jenner refused the offer. In total, Jenner received at least three proposals he turned down. Accepting those proposals would have meant leaving Berkeley and his family for many years.

When Jenner returned to Berkeley, his oldest brother, Reverend Stephen Jenner, resigned his position in Rockhampton, a nearby village. He took a position in Berkeley and moved in with Edward in their home town.

Starting His Practice

After moving into his new home, Edward Jenner focused on establishing his medical practice. For this, he had to let everybody in town know that a new doctor had arrived and was offering his services. This probably did not take a long time, because Jenner and his family were well-known in the area. As soon as the people in town knew that the Jenner brothers were moving in, they probably spread the word among friends and neighbors. Many citizens and farmers probably remembered Jenner from the time he was a student in grammar school. Jenner's easygoing and friendly character probably opened many doors for him.

A few of Jenner's patients came to his home for treatment. But most of the time he was on call. He often traveled on horseback, regardless of the weather. He went from farm to farm responding to his patients' calls. It was not uncommon for Jenner to spend the night or even a few days at the patient's home. It seems Jenner provided his services over an area of about one thousand square kilometers (four hundred square miles). This is as big as the city of San Antonio, Texas. He charged his patients according to how far he had to travel, regardless of the nature of the call.

As a family doctor, Jenner had various duties. He would take care of stomach pains and fevers. He would treat cuts, sprains, and other minor injuries. As a doctor, Jenner would handle minor procedures—such as suturing, or sewing, injured arms or legs. But he also had to perform major operations.

Once, he received an emergency call to operate on a strangulated hernia. A hernia is a protrusion, or projection, of an organ through the wall of the abdomen, and it can be fatal. Jenner had to place the protruding organ back in the abdomen and close the opening. But during this delicate operation the patient vomited, and all his intestines spilled out through the opening. Nobody expected the man to survive after this, but Jenner managed to restore the organs to their right place, and the patient lived for many years after the operation. Even in the twenty-first century this would be considered a very difficult and dangerous operation. Jenner was definitely a well-trained doctor.

Soon the experience Jenner had gained in London became obvious to his fellow doctors. They frequently sought his opinion, asking him for advice on difficult cases. These consultations took place at Jenner's office at home, and also during special social gatherings.

Meeting with Colleagues

Jenner met with other doctors and friends in public places such as the Ship Inn. During their meetings they discussed medical cases or topics of general interest to the community, such as taxes or the rise of prices. The meetings were more an occasion for eating, drinking, and having a good time among friends than for serious scientific discussions.

A typical meeting began with the reading of a "paper" or a presentation, followed by a discussion. Then, everybody enjoyed a good meal, and the meeting ended with songs, choruses, and poems. The meetings appealed very much to Jenner. He enjoyed both the discussions and gathering with friends for a good meal and a night of live entertainment. His friends said he had a good sense of humor, "which he liked to spread around."[1] Jenner would play the flute or the violin, recite verses of his own composition, and even sing.

There is an anecdote about Jenner during one of these meetings. It clearly shows that he liked to use the scientific methods of observation and experimentation to solve problems. The anecdote goes like this: During one of the gatherings the guests were served a dish that needed to be warmed up by a candle. They began to discuss whether the dish should be placed directly in the flame of the candle or a little above it. Jenner placed his finger in the flame and held it there for a little while. Then he put his finger

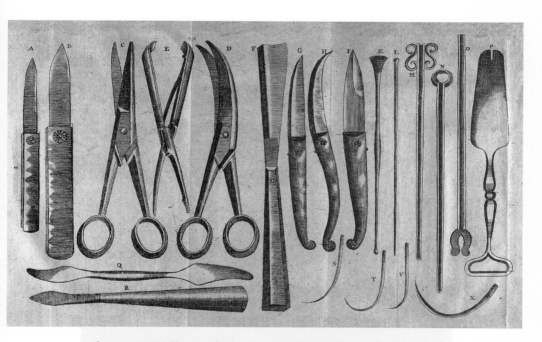

Jenner usually carried a case with a basic set of surgical instruments called "pocket instruments." A and B are lancets like the ones Jenner used to inoculate and vaccinate against smallpox. The instruments in this drawing from 1748 were made of steel, ivory, silver, or whalebone.

above the flame but withdrew it immediately. "There gentlemen," he said. "The question is answered."[2]

Between 1772 and 1778 Jenner dedicated his time not only to his medical practice but also to the observation of natural phenomena. His former tutor John Hunter wrote him many letters encouraging him to pursue numerous experiments. Hunter was particularly interested in the study of the hibernation of hedgehogs. He asked Jenner to send him live hedgehogs to study in London, where there were no hedgehogs. Hunter also asked Jenner to carry out experiments.

Hedgehogs

How hedgehogs hibernate was then a mystery. For many weeks these small mammals—covered with small, sharp spines—did not eat or come out of their burrow. Jenner did experiments to discover how they did it.

Jenner measured the hedgehog's body temperature and weight before and after hibernation. He discovered that one way these animals manage to survive the winter is by lowering their body temperature. When they get colder, all body functions—such as breathing, heartbeat, and digestion—slow down. The hedgehogs look as if they are dead. They don't move or eat for weeks, yet they are alive. Once, Jenner tried to wake one hedgehog up by dropping him on the ground. The little prickly creature bounced around and went on sleeping as though nothing had happened!

Jenner realized that the hedgehogs were not dead. Their bodies did not stop working completely during hibernation. Their bodies just slowed down. One proof of this was that the animals lost weight during their long sleep. If their bodies had completely stopped functioning, their body weight at the beginning of hibernation would have been the same as it was at the end. Jenner weighed the hedgehogs and proved that after hibernation the hedgehogs were lighter than before hibernation. Today we know that not only hedgehogs but other animals, such as bears, also hibernate to survive long winters, when food is scarce. But in the 1700s nobody knew what happened to the hedgehogs during winter. Thanks in part to Jenner's experiments, Hunter wrote a paper on hedgehogs and was accepted as a Fellow of the Royal Society.

After Jenner, other scientists continued studying hedgehogs and learned how they prepare for hibernation by feasting on their favorite foods, like the worm. They also eat insects and forage on grasses.

John Hunter constantly encouraged Jenner to pursue natural studies on his own so that he could one day write a paper to the Royal Society and become one of its prestigious members. But Jenner was in no hurry to acquire fame. He seemed to be content practicing medicine, collecting samples, and doing experiments in collaboration with Hunter.

An Epidemic

It seems that during the first six years following Jenner's return to Berkeley, his interest in cowpox remained dormant. However, in 1778 a very important local event rekindled Jenner's interest in the cow disease. In 1778 a smallpox epidemic struck Berkeley and its surrounding areas. This tragedy broke the familiar routine Jenner had enjoyed since his arrival in Berkeley.[3]

The deadly disease had come back again after its last visit ten years earlier. Many children had been born in those ten years, and none had been exposed to smallpox. They were the most likely victims of the speckled monster. As the country doctor, Jenner came face-to-face with the most deadly health threat of the time.

During the epidemic Jenner inoculated children to protect them from the virulent smallpox infection. He must have remembered the traumatic experience he went through when Mr. Holbrow inoculated him when he was eight years old. He probably heard again milkmaids saying they could "not take the smallpox because they had already had the cowpox." All these experiences during the 1778 epidemic quite probably compelled Jenner to find out how cowpox protected against smallpox.

He began his observations by testing whether what the milkmaids said was true. He inoculated milkmaids who had had the cowpox and observed if they got smallpox. Jenner was pleased to see that some milkmaids did not contract the disease. But he was puzzled when some milkmaids who had had cowpox got sick with smallpox. Why did cowpox protect against smallpox in some cases but not in others? Jenner knew that he had to do more experiments to find the answer.

5

On Bony Canals and Hydrogen Balloons

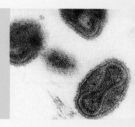

DURING THE 1778 SMALLPOX EPIDEMIC Jenner realized that studying how cowpox protected against smallpox was not as easy as finding out which part of the candle is the hottest, as he had done during one of his social meetings. To begin with, Jenner was puzzled by the fact that cowpox protected some of the milkmaids against smallpox, but it did not protect others.

He applied the scientific tools of observation and experimentation to solve the cowpox puzzle. However, it took him many years to figure it out. One of the main reasons was that cowpox was a very elusive disease. It was hard to find cases of cowpox frequently enough to do the necessary observations and experiments.

The cows in the dairies of Berkeley and the areas close by were not always sick with cowpox. For years not one of the cows would get sick with cowpox, and then the next year many would suffer from it. Nobody knew where it came from or how cows contracted it. But the farmers knew that after a few weeks all the cows would recover and the cowpox would be gone again for perhaps a few years.

Jenner was aware of this, and he knew that when there was an outbreak of cowpox at the dairies, this would be his only chance to observe and experiment. Once cowpox was gone, he would have to wait till the next epidemic.

Something similar happened with smallpox. A smallpox epidemic would only happen every few years. Once an epidemic was over, smallpox might not be seen again for as many as five—or sometimes even fifteen—years. Jenner could only do his observations and experiments when the disease was present. It is different today, though. Scientists have overcome this problem by learning how to grow the germs in the laboratory. In this way they have a constant supply of germs for their experiments.

Angina Pectoris

While waiting for the pox diseases to reappear, Jenner was not idle. Besides taking care of his patients, he took an interest in another medical problem of importance at the time, as it is today. Its name is *angina pectoris*, or chest angina, and his friend John Hunter suffered from it.

Hunter experienced pain in his chest now and then. Once it was so severe that he felt dizzy for two days and had to stay in bed. Jenner worried about his old friend. He probably wondered what could be causing him so much pain.

If studying cowpox was difficult to do in Jenner's time, studying angina pectoris was no lesser challenge. The only way for Jenner to know what

Portrait of Edward Jenner by Sir Thomas Laurence.

caused angina pectoris was to see what was going on inside a patient's heart and blood vessels. Jenner had the opportunity to have a closer look on a few occasions.

After a patient had died of angina pectoris, a disease marked by the attacks of severe chest pain, Jenner obtained permission from the family to look at the heart and blood vessels. He observed something no other doctor of his time had reported before. He saw a whitish substance narrowing or blocking the vessels that bring blood to the heart. The substance made the vessels hard, instead of soft and flexible as they are in young people. Jenner was so surprised to see this hard white substance in the vessel that at first he thought it had fallen from the plastered ceiling above him.[1]

He wrote to his colleague Dr. Caleb Hillier Parry: "I was making a transverse section [cut] of the heart pretty near its base, when my knife struck against something so hard and gritty, as to notch it. I well remember looking up to the ceiling, which was old and crumbling, conceiving that some plaster had fallen down. But on a further scrutiny the real cause appeared: the coronary's [blood vessels] were become bony canals."[2]

Jenner understood that the cause of death, as well as the pain, was the blockage of the blood vessels. The blockage prevented the heart from receiving enough blood and oxygen, and it stopped working. Although it was an important discovery, Jenner did not want to publish it. He did not want the "dear man," as he called Hunter, to know that he had a disease for which there was no cure. Hunter died of a severe angina pectoris attack years later.

Flying High

Jenner's interests reached past the medical field. In 1785 he and his friend Edward Gardner built one of the first, if not the first, manmade flying machines in England—a hydrogen balloon. Word had reached Jenner that the Montgolfier brothers in France had built a balloon that could fly many meters above the ground. So he decided to build one and see if it could fly, as the one in France did.

Jenner must have been very excited about this experiment. He wrote to a friend and joked about preparing a distraction with firecrackers to cover his escape in case the balloon did not rise in front of the crowd. He wrote to Dr. Caleb Hillier Parry: "Should it [the balloon] prove unwillingly to mount & turn shy before a large Assembly, don't you think I may make my escape under cover of three or four dozen Squib & Crackers [firecrackers]?"[3]

Jenner's balloon flew nicely twice over the Valley of Severn. The second time he released it from the town of Kingscote. It flew without a passenger, but it carried a poem, perhaps for good luck. The end of the poem went like this:

> My flight I took from Kingscote's happy plain,
> A daring wand'rer through the ethereal sky;
> Then, gentle friend, pray take me back again,
> Perhaps, once more, another course to try.[4]

J. Charles and M. Robert filled the first hydrogen balloon in Paris, France in 1783. They produced hydrogen gas by pouring sulfuric acid upon iron filings. Jenner used this procedure to fill his balloons.

Some say that Jenner may have planned this on purpose to have the chance to go to Kingscote and meet Catherine Kingscote, his future wife.

Jenner had a zest for experimentation, and defeat did not dim his enthusiasm. While he waited for cowpox and smallpox to come back, his endless curiosity led him to solve another mystery, the mystery of the cuckoo bird. And his endless sense of duty almost got him killed.

6

Of the Blizzard and Cuckoo Birds

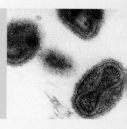

THE YEAR 1786 WAS ROUGH ON EDWARD Jenner. First, he came down with a severe illness called typhoid fever. For days he had very high fever and vomited many times. He recovered, but it took many weeks for him to fully regain his strength. After this illness he almost froze to death in a blizzard.

It was early in the year when he had to make a 16-kilometer (10-mile) ride to Kingscote, probably to see a patient. The air was very cold, more cold "than I ever remember to have experienced it." Although it should not have taken him too long under clear weather to ride the 16 kilometers, the storm delayed his trip considerably. "The ground was deeply covered in snow and it blew a hurricane accompanied with continual snow."[1]

He was not worried about his situation until he began ascending the hills. Then he could not feel his body; the extreme cold had numbed him. "There was no possibility of keeping the snow from driving under my hat, so that half my face and neck was, for a long time, wrapt in ice."

Despite the life-threatening circumstances, Jenner did not lose his sense of humor. "I felt like . . . one intoxicated [drunk], and could not forebear [stop] singing." But his situation was very serious indeed. "My hands at last grew extremely painful. . . . When I came to the horse I was unable to dismount without assistance. I was almost senseless; but I had just recollection and power enough to prevent the servants from bringing me to the fire." Jenner knew that to avoid further pain, his body had to warm up slowly. He began his recovery in the stables, away from the fireplace. He was lucky that day. He fully recovered after the experience, "but a man perished a few miles from Kingscote, at the same time and from the same cause."[2]

The year 1786 got better for Jenner after these early misfortunes. In the spring he made his final observations and experiments on a topic that granted him membership in the prestigious Royal Society. He unraveled the mystery of the cuckoo bird, in which he had been interested ever since his return from London in 1772.

Observing the Cuckoo

Cuckoo birds are different from other birds in that they do not make their own nests. The mother cuckoo lays her eggs in other birds' nests that already carry their own eggs. Then the cuckoo mother leaves. The "foster parents" raise the cuckoo chick as if it were their own baby. The foster parents' chicks or eggs are thrown out of the nest. And this was the mystery during Jenner's time. Nobody knew who had thrown the eggs or chicks out of the nest.

Some people thought that the foster parents removed their own eggs from the nest. But nobody had ever patiently watched to see what really happened to the eggs. This is exactly what Jenner did.

Every year around April cuckoo birds migrate to England to reproduce. Jenner knew they had arrived when he heard them singing. Then he began his observations. He confirmed that the cuckoo chick usually hatched before the other eggs in the nest, such as sparrow or reed warbler eggs.

He also confirmed that within one or two days after the cuckoo chick had hatched, the other eggs or chicks would be thrown out of the nest. The eggs or chicks never made it back to the nest. Predators such as mice or foxes usually ate them. But who had thrown the eggs and chicks out of their rightful home? The parents seemed to be the only ones capable of doing it. The cuckoo chick was just hatched. It didn't seem to have enough strength yet. He had to do more observations to solve this puzzle.

The day Jenner discovered how the foster parents' eggs disappeared from the nest, he was

Dr. R. Kilner in England has continued Jenner's studies on the cuckoo and discovered in 1999 that cuckoo chicks trick mother warblers into thinking she is feeding her own babies by making as much noise as all the little warblers in her nest.

observing a sparrow's nest built on the edge of a hedge. He could "distinctly see what was going forward in it." What he saw left him astonished. The newly hatched cuckoo had pushed the sparrow eggs out of the nest. [3]

The cuckoo chick had not even opened his eyes when he used his rump and wings to get the sparrow egg on his back. Clumsily, the cuckoo chick "clambered backwards with it [the egg] up the side of the nest till it reached the top, where, resting for a moment, it threw off his load with a jerk."[4]

Through the years 1786 and 1787, Jenner confirmed many times that the cuckoo chick was the one dumping the other eggs and chicks out of the nest. He wrote a report to the Royal Society in December 1787. The society accepted the report and a year later granted Jenner membership for this original research.

Becoming a Fellow of the Royal Society was a great achievement for Jenner. It meant that the scientific community had recognized him as an accomplished scientist. Being a member of the

Royal Society would be a very important credential later, when he began promoting cowpox as a safe way to protect people against smallpox.

Starting a Family

In 1788 Jenner made an important change in his life. He married Catherine Kingscote, who carried the name of the nearby village. The newlyweds moved into a two-story house Jenner had bought the year before. They called it The Chantry. In this fifteen-room home, Edward and Catherine lived happily for many years. They had two sons, Edward and Robert, and one daughter, Catherine.

Jenner's correspondence with John Hunter continued. His old mentor was very pleased when he finally wrote the report on the cuckoo's behavior. However, Hunter thought that Jenner took too long to finish his experiments and write a report. To this, Jenner answered that he could not dedicate all his time to his research. He was a country doctor and had to take care of his patients as well as family business. Jenner wrote to his friend and colleague Sir Joseph Banks, "A person engaged in business cannot conduct these matters [research] as he would wish; his pursuits are too often interrupted."[5]

However, Jenner also admitted that he might be lazy sometimes. He had medical responsibilities, took care of his family business, and enjoyed an active social life. He seems to have postponed his research more than necessary sometimes. He wrote to John Flinch, "of all the ill habits a man may fall into, indolence [laziness] is the most difficult to get rid of. I for one am a sad example of the truth of this position."[6]

In 1788 another smallpox epidemic threatened Berkeley. Jenner again confronted the speckled monster. This time it was threatening the life of his own son.

7

The Milkmaid's Fortune Is Her Face

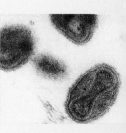

IN 1788 THE SPECKLED MONSTER threatened Berkeley one more time. Again the most probable victims of the monster would be the children who were born between two epidemics. None of them had been exposed to the deadly smallpox virus before. Their bodies had no defenses against the variola.

One of the children born between the epidemics was Jenner's first son, also named Edward. In 1789, when Edward Jr. was ten months old, smallpox was still present in the Valley of Severn. Unfortunately, it seems there was not one case of cowpox in the valley at the same time. Jenner could not reach for cowpox to try to protect his son. His memories of the consequences of the dreadful disease must have prompted him to try something else to protect him.

In November 1789 Jenner and his family were spending a few days in a nearby health spa, or medicinal baths, located in the neighborhood of Cheltenham. While they were at the spa a few people fell ill with a disease that looked a lot like a mild case of smallpox. They called it swine, or pig, pox. It seems that these people had been close to pigs sick with swine pox and had caught it. It is not clear today if this was really swine pox or a very mild case of smallpox.

Regardless of what it really was, Jenner saw the opportunity to protect his son and others who had not had smallpox before. He might have thought that if a cow disease that looks like smallpox can protect people against smallpox, then maybe a pig disease that looks like smallpox can also protect against the speckled monster. He inoculated his son, Edward, and two young servants with swine pox. Later on he inoculated them with smallpox virus, and they did not get the disease. It had worked.

How?

Years later, many people criticized Jenner for experimenting on his own son. How could he do this to his baby boy? People today would not do what Jenner did, because there are safe vaccines that protect against diseases. But in 1789 there was only one thing Jenner could do to try to protect his son against smallpox: He could inoculate him with a milder disease that looked like the speckled monster. He knew this had worked many times with cowpox. It was probably a hard decision for Jenner. However, it was not a reckless decision. He knew that his son probably would not die from a milder disease such as swine pox. But there was a high chance he would die from severe smallpox.

Cowpox

The reappearance of smallpox in the Valley of Severn gave Jenner a new opportunity to study the disease. He confirmed one more time that cowpox protected against smallpox in some cases, but not in others. What was the difference?

He asked the milkmaids questions about cowpox. How had they caught it? What did it look like in people and in cows? Where had it come from?

A milkmaid would catch cowpox while she was milking a cow suffering from the disease. The cow would have pus-filled pustules on her udders or teats. As she milked the cow some pustules would break, and the pus would get into a scratch or cut on the milkmaid's hands.[1] It was common for a milkmaid to have scratches on her hands. Besides milking the cows, she had to tend the garden, and a thorn might cut her skin.

A few days after getting infected by the pus, the milkmaid would have a mild fever and pustules would begin to appear on her hands. After seven to ten days, she would recover without any scars. She would now be protected from smallpox.

The milkmaids were not afraid of getting cowpox. They believed it would protect them from smallpox. And being protected from smallpox would save them from having a scarred face. They would be pretty, with a smooth, clear skin free of smallpox marks. "My face is my fortune," a milkmaid's song said.

Cowpox, a disease of cows, could only be found in the British Isles and some western European countries. The cows would get red, swollen rashes with bluish pustules in the middle. The animals would have a mild fever, become restless, and give less milk for a few days. But that would be the worst of it. After this, their temperature and milk production would go back to normal and the pustules would dry up and fall off.[2]

Nobody knew where cowpox came from. It seemed to appear and disappear from the dairies without a pattern. Jenner thought that cowpox was related to a disease of horses called "grease." He thought that stableboys who took care of horses and milked the cows sometimes brought the grease to the cows after handling a sick horse. But Jenner never found enough

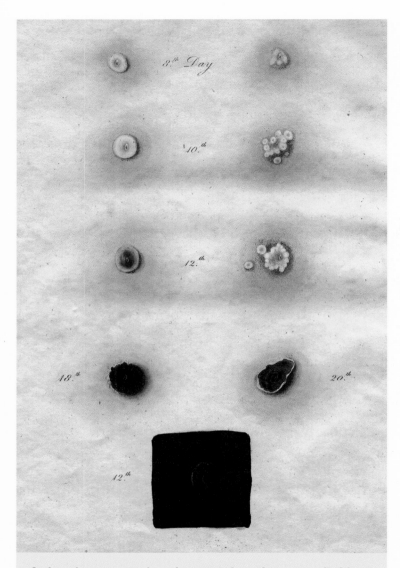

A drawing comparing the pustules of cowpox (left) and smallpox (right) at different times during the progression of the diseases.

evidence to prove that cowpox and grease were related.[3]

Jenner found the cowpox puzzle really hard to solve. He decided to bring his observations to the meetings of the new Gloucester Medical Society, which he had founded with a few colleagues in 1788.

Reaction from the Medical Community

Jenner thought his fellow doctors would help him solve the puzzle. But to his disappointment his colleagues were not interested in the cowpox puzzle at all. They thought it was just superstition. Some called it "an old wives' tale," meaning it was not true.

Their skepticism was understandable. After all, if cowpox protected against smallpox, then all of the milkmaids that ever had cowpox would never get smallpox. But it did not work all the time. So it could not be cowpox that protected against smallpox. It must have been something else. And who had ever heard of a cow disease protecting against a human disease? It made no sense at all.

To eighteenth-century doctors, the idea that something in the pus of a cowpox pustule could protect against any other disease was unheard of. It was absurd. Doctors did not know about germs and how they can make people sick. They thought that bad smells from sick people or even magic spells caused diseases.

Jenner's opponents made fun of him and of the cowpox vaccine with caricatures. This one shows Jenner vaccinating people who then "bovinised" or grew cows out of their bodies.

Not even Jenner knew about germs. What Jenner knew was that in many cases having cowpox was a safe way to be protected against deadly smallpox. It really worked. So he did not dismiss cowpox as easily as his colleagues did. He looked at the cowpox puzzle in a different way. He asked himself other questions instead. What makes cowpox work sometimes, but not always? What is the difference between a cowpox infection that works and one that does not?

In spite of the rejection by his colleagues, Jenner brought the cowpox puzzle up for discussion very often during gatherings of the medical society. In fact, he brought it up so frequently that his colleagues got tired of listening to it. They even threatened to bar him from the meetings unless he stopped talking about it! Jenner soon realized that he would have to solve the puzzle on his own.

Continuing Research

In 1791, the elusive cowpox reappeared in the dairies. Jenner must have been excited. He could now study cowpox firsthand and try to solve the puzzle. He focused his study on the pustules of the disease, both on cows' udders and on people's hands. Jenner even had an artist, Mr. Cuff, draw pictures of the pustules over the course of the disease.[4] In this way, he could study them over and over after the disease once again disappeared.

Jenner noticed that the pustules' appearance changed as the disease progressed. At the beginning, they were small. Then, they grew in size and filled up with pus. After this, the pustules became smaller and less red. Finally, they dried up and the scabs fell off, barely leaving a mark.

For months Jenner thought about the changes in the pustules. Could these changes be related to cowpox's ability to protect against smallpox? Jenner did not know it, but he was very close to making one of the most important medical discoveries of the eighteenth century. But for this he needed the collaboration of eight-year-old James Phipps.

James Phipps

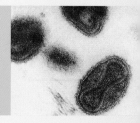

BETWEEN THE YEARS 1791 AND 1796, Jenner had a eureka moment and solved the cowpox puzzle. The years he had spent carefully observing the pustules on cows' udders and on the milkmaids' hands had finally paid off. He discovered how to make cowpox germs protect people against smallpox all the time.

First, Jenner realized that there was more than one cow disease that looked like cowpox. However, only one of them would protect against smallpox. Jenner called this true cowpox. He called the other types of rashes spurious, or false, cowpox, because they would not make a person immune to, or protected against, smallpox.[1]

Using the drawings of the pustules, Jenner learned to distinguish true cowpox from spurious diseases. In Jenner's words, true cowpox is the cow disease with pustules that look like "a section of a pearl on a rose leaf [petal]."[2]

The second part of the puzzle that Jenner solved was related to the pustules in true cowpox. He could not stop thinking about why the pustules changed their appearance as the disease progressed. At the beginning and at the end of the disease, the pustules were smaller and had less pus than halfway through the disease. In the middle of the disease period, the pustules were bigger and had a bluish, sunken center. It seemed to Jenner that the disease at the beginning and at the end was somewhat weaker than in the middle stage. Then he asked a key question: What if the small pustules are not strong enough to confer protection? What if only the largest bluish pustules are strong enough to protect against smallpox?[3]

Jenner did not know how to explain this. Furthermore, he did not have any experiment to prove it. How could he be sure that his idea was correct? He had to do an experiment. But, as had happened before, smallpox and cowpox disappeared from the valley between 1791 and 1796. Jenner had to wait again for their return.

Losing a Friend

The wait was not uneventful. In 1793 Jenner had to face the death of his "dear man," John Hunter. On August 12 Hunter collapsed at Saint George's Hospital and died after a severe attack

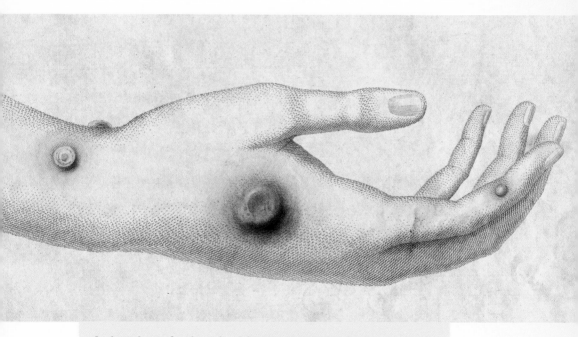

A drawing of a hand with cowpox pustules. Jenner would use material from such pustules for his smallpox vaccine.

of angina pectoris. This occurred after he had lost his temper in an argument with colleagues during a meeting.

As Jenner had discovered, angina pectoris is caused by blockage of the arteries that feed blood and oxygen to the heart. In time the heart weakens because it does not receive enough nutrients. When people get upset, as Hunter did, their blood pressure rises. If it gets too high and the heart is weak, then it might stop beating. And this is what ended John Hunter's life. In a way, Hunter was aware the weakness of his heart might kill him one day. He wrote once, "My life is in the hands of any fool who cares to upset me."[4]

Between 1794 and 1796, Jenner probably had much time on his hands to think about the cowpox puzzle. At the end of 1794, he thought he had a cold, but it turned out to be another severe attack of typhoid fever. He had to stay in bed for weeks, and also to reduce his usual activities for many months. Typhoid fever was a common disease at the time. His wife,

Catherine, had also had it, as well as Jenner's sister-in-law and nephews.

In the summer of 1795, the Jenner family moved to Cheltenham to recover their strength in the medicinal, warm waters of the spa. Slowly Jenner resumed his medical practice, had social gatherings at his home, and returned to the meetings of the Gloucester Medical Society.

Playing Detective

In April 1796 Jenner had another opportunity to put into practice his scientific skills. This time he helped solve a murder case. A man called William Reed had died after suffering severe stomach pains and vomiting. Jenner's nephew Henry, who was also a doctor, thought the circumstances of the man's death were suspicious and gave some of Reed's vomit to a dog. The dog quickly died.

Henry asked his uncle to analyze Reed's stomach contents. Jenner discovered two poisons in the stomach, arsenic and mercury. In the meantime, Reed's wife left town in a hurry. Jenner told the authorities about the poisons he had found in Reed's stomach. The police captured Mrs. Reed, and she was tried and found guilty of murder.[5]

The Return of Cowpox

In 1796 cowpox and smallpox were back in the valley. The time had come for Edward Jenner to finally test his idea that cowpox would only protect from smallpox when the pus was taken from the "strongest" pustules.

Jenner had carefully thought about how he would do the experiment. First, he would find a milkmaid with cowpox. When the milkmaid's pustules were the right size and color, he would transfer the pus to a healthy person who had never had either cowpox or smallpox. The best candidate would be a child. Jenner chose eight-year-old James Phipps. He was the son of a worker who often provided his services to the Jenner family.[6]

In May 1796 a young milkmaid named Sarah Nelmes caught cowpox. She was milking a sick cow called Blossom when some of the pus entered her body through a thorn scratch on her hand. Jenner closely observed the development of cowpox on Sarah. It would be a matter of a few days until some of her pustules became strong enough to confer protection.

On May 14, 1796, James Phipps held out his arm to Jenner. Jenner took a lancet, which looks like a small, sharp knife, and made two incisions, or cuts, "each about half an inch long" on James's left arm.[7] Then using the tip of a clean lancet, Jenner slightly cut the large pustule on Sarah's hand, taking some of the pus. He placed the pale pus into the incisions on James's arm and wrapped it with a clean bandage. Now they had to wait.

Four days later, the incisions on James's arm became red. After four more days two pustules with "reddish raised edges and a bluish sunken center" appeared around the incisions.[8] James felt weak and had a fever for the next couple of days and then he felt well again.

James had successfully caught cowpox from another person, but the test was not over yet.

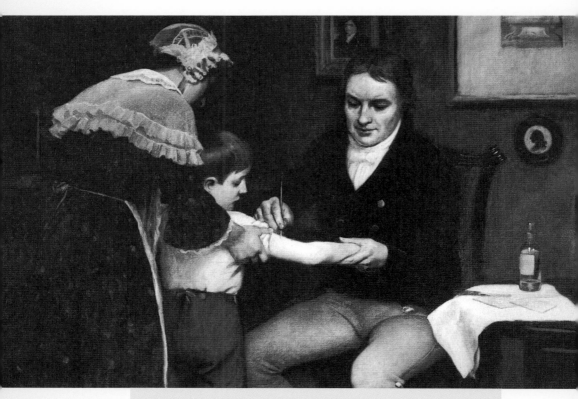

**Jenner vaccinates James Phipps on May 14, 1796—
the first safe vaccination against deadly smallpox.**

Would he be immune to, or protected against, smallpox? To test this, Jenner infected James with smallpox on July 1, but he did not "take the smallpox."

Jenner was really excited about the results. He wrote to his friend Edward Gardner: "But listen to the most delightful part of my story. The boy has since been inoculated for the small pox which as I ventured to predict produc'd no effect. I shall now pursue my experiments with redoubled ardor."[9]

Jenner had finally solved the cowpox puzzle. He had discovered for the first time how to protect people safely against a deadly disease.

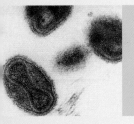

The Inquiry

IN 1797 JENNER WROTE A DETAILED report to the Royal Society. In this report he described the experiment with James Phipps and how cowpox had provided him immunity to smallpox. Jenner also described the case stories of thirteen other individuals who had been naturally infected with cowpox while milking cows and did not get smallpox either.

On July 10 Jenner sent the report to the Royal Society. Sir Everard Home took the report and showed it to the members of the society. He sent it back to Jenner with a note stating that "it did not merit publication because of insufficient data."[1]

The members felt that conducting just one experiment, the one with James Phipps, was not enough evidence to prove that cowpox was a safe way to protect people against smallpox. They were right about this. Scientists then, just as today, had to repeat an experiment many times to confirm that a new medical procedure worked and was safe before using it on a large number people. However, this was not the only reason to reject Jenner's report.

In the members' minds and in the minds of many doctors of the time, the milkmaids' belief was still no better than superstition. They asked Jenner to forget about it if he wanted other doctors to respect him. They told Jenner that he "would more likely keep his colleagues' esteem in this respectable society by withdrawing his manuscript and forgetting about it as quickly as possible."[2]

Not Giving Up

Did Jenner give up and forgot about cowpox? On the contrary, he pursued the matter even further. He decided to repeat the experiment he had performed on James Phipps with other children. Jenner could not perform the experiment on adults. He needed people who had never had cowpox or smallpox. Most adults had already had one disease or the other and were protected. But most children were not.

Cowpox and smallpox were absent from the valley again. Fortunately for Jenner, he did not have to wait too long this time. In February 1798 cowpox returned to the dairies, and Jenner repeated his experiments.

On March 16, 1798, Jenner passed on pus from a cow carrying true cowpox to five-year-old William Summers. On March 28 Jenner used the arm-to-arm transfer to transmit cowpox from William Summers to William Pead. On April 15 William Pead provided the material for transmitting cowpox to seven-year-old Hannah Excell.

Jenner used material from Hannah's pustules to infect four more children, including his eleven-month-old son, Robert. Unfortunately, the vaccine did not work on Robert. However, it worked on three other children, J. Macklove, M. James, and Mary Pead.

Jenner continued the arm-to-arm transfer from Mary Pead to a seven-year-old boy named J. Barge. All the children contracted a mild case of cowpox, with the exception of Robert Jenner.[3] These experiments showed Jenner that he did not need to have cows sick with cowpox to transmit the disease to people. He could transmit it equally as well by using the arm-to-arm transfer. He had done it successfully up to six times. This was important because it meant that he no longer depended on having cows with cowpox. He could still protect against smallpox as long as he kept on passing cowpox from person to person.

Jenner later infected the children with smallpox and confirmed that they were protected against it. The procedure Jenner had devised worked! He now rewrote his original report, including the new results.

Jenner gave his report a long name, *An Inquiry into the Causes and Effects of the Variola Vaccinae, a Disease Discovered in Some of the Western Countries of England, Particularly Gloucestershire and Known by the Name of Cowpox*. Naturally, everybody called it *The Inquiry*, for short.

Publishing His Findings

Jenner decided not to send it again to the Royal Society. This time he paid a London printer, Sampson Low, to publish it. The original had seventy-five pages and four color plates showing the pustules on Sarah Nelmes's hands and on some of the children. It was published in June 1798. Jenner was forty-nine years old.

Two more editions of *The Inquiry* followed, in 1800 and 1801. The last edition was translated into German, French, Spanish, Dutch, Italian, and Latin. Jenner also published three more books: *Further Observations on the Variola Vaccinae, or Cow-pox* in 1799, *A Continuation of Facts and Observations Relative to Variola Vaccinae* in 1800, and *The Origin of Vaccine Inoculation* in 1801.

In his books Jenner not only described the experiments but also explained step-by-step the arm-to-arm procedure that would confer protection. The detailed instructions together with the illustrations would allow other doctors to differentiate true cowpox from the spurious diseases and perform the correct procedure.

Jenner also reported that the cowpox pus could be stored in "the shaft of a bird's feather and sealed with wax."[4] This was very important because it meant that doctors did not need a sick cow or person to protect against smallpox. They could collect the pus, store it in a feather, and proceed to pass on the protective fluid where it was needed. This was the best way they had at the time to preserve the cowpox fluid. Refrigeration had not been invented yet.

Jenner indicated that if doctors perfectly sealed the cowpox material, it would still confer protection after about three months of storage. However, if the sample got hot or wet, the material would lose its power to protect against smallpox.

Jenner pointed out the benefits his procedure had over inoculation, using a mild case of smallpox, which would confer protection against a severe case. However, a smallpox inoculation could be fatal, and people had to be quarantined until they recovered to avoid spreading the deadly disease. A cowpox infection also protected against smallpox, but it was much safer. It was never fatal, and people could return home to recover from it. Jenner's procedure received the new name "vaccination," inspired by

Mothers brought their young children to receive free vaccinations in Paris. A doctor vaccinates a baby while his assistant holds the vaccinating instruments. In the background, another assistant extracts cowpox matter from a cow.

the fact that it came from *vaccae*, or "cows" in Latin. The cowpox pus became a vaccine.

Public Reaction

The news of the wonderful procedure spread all over the world. Many doctors in England, Europe, America, and in the rest of the world read Jenner's publications with avid interest. They talked to each other and passed on the news.

Many doctors around the world followed the vaccination procedure carefully and succeeded in protecting their patients from smallpox. But others applied the technique carelessly and did not protect people. They said the procedure did not work. Others tried to discredit Jenner by making fun of cowpox. Some of his opponents said that people would start looking like cows if they received the cowpox material. Many people believed this and refused to be treated with cowpox.

Jenner's job was far from done. He knew cowpox worked. Now he had to go to London to convince others that it was true.

Conquering Smallpox

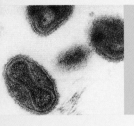

THE PUBLICATION OF *THE INQUIRY* changed Jenner's life forever. He would no longer be the country doctor who enjoyed visiting his patients and doing science experiments. He would no longer meet frequently with friends and colleagues at the local inn.

The publication of *The Inquiry* gave him a new purpose in life. Jenner had now to convince the world that his vaccine worked, and that it worked much better than inoculation.

The first London doctors to prove that Jenner's vaccination worked were his friends Henry Cline and Dr. Lister. Cline vaccinated an eight-year-old boy with a cowpox sample Jenner had given him in a feather shaft. The boy developed a mild case of cowpox and later on proved to be immune to smallpox. After the success of these London doctors, the news began to spread by word of mouth that vaccination was a safe way to prevent smallpox.[1]

The Campaign for Cowpox

Jenner worked very hard to get supporters for vaccination, but it took a greater effort to convince his opponents. The first obstacle Jenner found was that some doctors were careless and did not follow his method precisely. Some doctors did not take the time to compare the drawings of the true cowpox pustules with the pustules on a cow. Sometimes they vaccinated people with spurious cowpox instead of true cowpox, and those people did not develop immunity.

Other doctors were more careful and made sure they immunized with true cowpox. William Woodville of the London Smallpox Hospital, for example, asked a veterinarian called Tanner to use his expertise to identify true cowpox in a London dairy using Jenner's drawings.

Woodville then vaccinated many people with true cowpox—but he did not keep them separate from patients who already had smallpox. Woodville found that 60 percent of the people he vaccinated got smallpox rather than cowpox. He then claimed that vaccination did not work.[2]

Jenner was concerned about these results. They certainly did not help him in his campaign to win support for vaccination. But Jenner was not puzzled about the results. It was clear to him that the vaccine had not failed. It was Woodville who had made the mistake of keeping people who had just been vaccinated together in the same rooms and beds with others carrying smallpox. Vaccination does not work instantly. People had to come down with and recover from cowpox to give the body time to become immune to smallpox.

Jenner had to take a lot of time explaining to London doctors why they had to keep cowpox and smallpox patients separate. He also invested much of his time writing to doctors in other

The Jennerian Society for the Extermination of Smallpox was founded in London in 1803. It distributed Jenner's vaccine all over the world.

countries explaining the important details that make vaccination work. Jenner believed that smallpox inoculation should be banned and replaced with vaccination.

Opposition to Vaccination

Once the issue of contamination of cowpox-vaccinated patients with smallpox was addressed, Jenner faced two other types of opponents. First, there were those who thought that using cowpox to prevent smallpox was simply unnatural. They thought nothing good would come out of it. They claimed that people were going to "bovinise," or turn into cows. Dr. B. Moseley was one of those who fiercely opposed vaccination for this reason.[3] He even founded an antivaccination group that distributed cartoons ridiculing Jenner and vaccination.

Jenner also had to fight those who realized that his method worked and wanted to take credit for it. When Jenner visited London, his opponents tried to arrange public debates on vaccination. However, Jenner never participated in direct discussions between himself and his opponents. He did not want to be placed in a position where he could be insulted or ridiculed.

Between 1798 and 1823, Jenner focused on defending and promoting vaccination. He spent all his time writing letters, holding conferences, and talking to people. He did not have time to practice medicine anymore, let alone perform any experiments. Because he was not seeing any patients, he did not earn any money. He lived on his savings, but soon he was running out of money.

In London's Smallpox Vaccination Hospital, doctors took care of smallpox patients and provided vaccinations. Jenner pointed out that it was mandatory to separate smallpox patients from vaccinated people to prevent infection with smallpox before the vaccine triggered immunity.

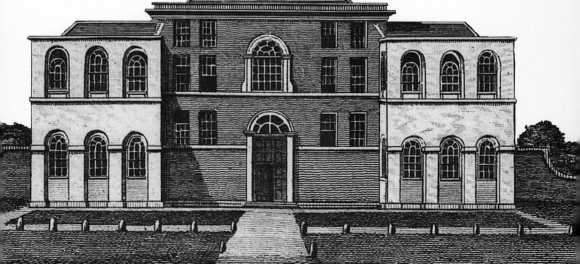

Some of his friends advised him to request a grant from the king of England, George III. It was not exceptional for people who had provided a valuable service to the community to request a grant from the king. The grant would compensate them for the money that had been spent while they were working on their discovery. Jenner received two grants. The first one in 1802 was for ten thousand pounds, and the second one in 1806 for twenty thousand pounds.[4]

The World Reacts

All over the world, from Europe to Asia to recently independent America, people benefited from Jenner's vaccine. Within about four years of the publication of *The Inquiry*, he had become famous and respected in a large part of the world as one of the greatest benefactors of humanity. He had discovered the means to defeat the speckled monster of smallpox.

Even well-known political figures of the time admired and respected Edward Jenner. Enemies of England, such as Napoleon Bonaparte, thought Jenner deserved their respect and consideration. In 1804 Dr. Williams and Dr. Wickham, two supporters of vaccination and friends of Jenner's, were prisoners in France because of a war between the two countries. Jenner decided to write a letter to the leader of France, Napoleon. In this letter Jenner requested his friends' release. He argued that even though their countries were at war, "the sciences are never at war."

History relates that Napoleon responded, "Jenner—we can't refuse that man anything."[5] William and Wickham received safe passage back to England.

Jenner's fame brought him many honors, mostly medals, diplomas, and a few cash awards in addition to the grants from the British crown. One important honor for Jenner was the degree of doctor of medicine from the University of Oxford in 1813. This was a great honor considering that Oxford had not conferred an honorary degree in medicine on anyone for about seventy years. Jenner's portrait has appeared on commemorative stamps. Even a crater on the moon has his name![6]

Tragedy

Sadly, tragedy darkened Jenner's success. His wife, Catherine, died in 1815. She had rarely enjoyed good health in spite of Jenner's care and the visits to Cheltenham spa. After her death Jenner never left Berkeley again. From his home, he continued vaccinating people and responding to the never-ending letters. In the backyard of The Chantry, Jenner had a one-room hut. People called it The Temple of Vaccinia. In this hut, every Thursday morning Jenner vaccinated for free all who came.

After Catherine died, Jenner's health slowly deteriorated. He always felt very tired. On January 25, 1823, a servant found him lying unconscious on the floor of his library. James Phipps, now about thirty-five years old, fetched Jenner's friends and family. Jenner regained consciousness, but did not leave his bed. He died the next day at about 2:00 A.M. His family buried him in the church of Berkeley. He rests there today, surrounded by his wife and children.

Jenner gave to the world the weapon that would destroy the monster everybody thought was unstoppable. Jenner knew that with his vaccine the speckled monster could be stopped on its destructive path forever, saving millions of lives. His dream took about 180 years to come true, though—from 1796, when James Phipps from England became the first person to be vaccinated, until 1977, when Ali Maow Maalin from Somalia became the last victim of the speckled monster.

The Last Case of Smallpox

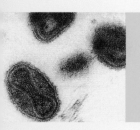

JENNER PREDICTED THAT VACCINATION would lead to the eradication, or complete elimination, of smallpox about 180 years before it happened. He wrote in the last paragraph of his book *The Origin of the Vaccine Inoculation*: "The annihilation of the small pox, the most dreadful scourge of the human species, must be the final result of this practice [vaccination]."

Using Jenner's vaccine, doctors led numerous vaccination campaigns to eliminate smallpox. The largest effort to spread vaccination in the nineteenth century was sponsored by King Charles IV of Spain in 1803.[1]

Dr. Francisco Xavier Balmis commanded La Real Expedición Marítima de la Vacuna or "The Royal Maritime Vaccination Expedition."

The expedition traveled through all the Spanish colonies in North, Central, and South America and in the Philippines for three years. They successfully vaccinated tens of thousands of people using the arm-to-arm transfer.

Nobody had found cowpox in the New World or in the Philippines, so Balmis had to bring Jenner's vaccine from Spain. However, Balmis could not carry the vaccine in a sealed feather shaft, as Jenner had done before. The hot and humid tropical weather spoiled it. The only way he could carry the vaccine was in the bodies of people who had never had cowpox or smallpox. Balmis carried the vaccine in the bodies of orphan boys, passing it from one to the next using the arm-to-arm transfer as they traveled through the colonies.

Jenner was very pleased when he read of the success of the Spanish expedition. He wished the British crown had undertaken a similar vaccination campaign. Jenner wrote to Dr. Alexander Marcet in 1806, "Would to Heaven the British Cabinet had shewn [shown] the same Philanthropic Spirit as that of Spain."[2]

Vaccination Continues

After Jenner's death, vaccination against smallpox continued all over the world. However, in spite of the continuous vaccination efforts, the speckled monster persisted.

One of the reasons smallpox could not be eliminated quickly was that in many parts of the world some people still preferred to be inoculated instead of safely vaccinated. Using a mild case of smallpox instead of the vaccine assured that the speckled monster would always be present somewhere in the world, causing new outbreaks. The practice of inoculation continued even through relatively recent times. The last known inoculation was recorded in the Bale Province in southern Ethiopia in August 1976. It was associated with the last smallpox outbreak in the country.[3]

Besides a persistent inoculation practice, there were other reasons why smallpox survived till the second half of the twentieth century. Jenner believed that vaccinating with cowpox would provide a lifelong immunity against smallpox.

But he was wrong about this. Cowpox provides immunity for about six years. To be protected longer, people need another dose of cowpox to boost immunity and protect them from smallpox for a few more years. Until doctors realized that a booster was necessary, many people who had been vaccinated contracted smallpox anyway and passed it on to other people.

It was also necessary to develop better methods to prevent the vaccine from spoiling under the hottest and most humid weather conditions. Again, it was not until the first half of the twentieth century that scientists developed a freeze-dried vaccine. This vaccine would not spoil even without refrigeration.[4]

The End of Smallpox

In 1967 humanity was ready to confront and defeat smallpox once and for all. In that year the World Health Organization (WHO), which is made up of members from countries all over the world, decided to begin a smallpox eradication campaign. It took ten years of

Edward Jenner: Conqueror of Smallpox

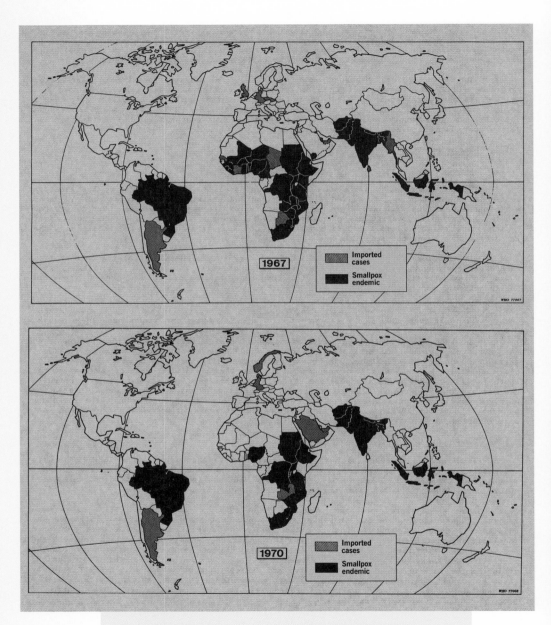

1967

Imported cases

Smallpox endemic

1970

Imported cases

Smallpox endemic

During the ten years of the W.H.O. eradication campaign, the "speckled monster" of smallpox slowly disappeared from the world.

nonstop vaccinations and watching for new cases to defeat it. Finally, in 1977 the speckled monster made its last stand in the city of Marka, located in Somalia in the Horn of Africa.[5]

On May 8, 1980, WHO officially announced the eradication of smallpox. The news made the headlines of major newspapers. The *New York Times* said, ERADICATION OF SMALLPOX TO BE ANNOUNCED TODAY. The *Washington Post* announced, TOTAL VICTORY IN TWO-CENTURY EFFORT IS PROCLAIMED BY SMALLPOX WARRIORS.

One of the major obstacles during the eradication campaign was that many people did not want to be vaccinated. Many preferred traditional inoculation, which had been used for hundreds of years, instead of the new method of vaccination. They might have even thought they would bovinise, or turn into cows, as Jenner's enemies had claimed a century before. Ali Maow Maalin was one of the people who did not want to be vaccinated. He remembers how he caught smallpox in 1977.

The Last Case of Smallpox

Ali was a health worker in his hometown of Marka, Somalia. He recalls when the authorities in his town began vaccinating people against smallpox. Even though his job was to help provide vaccinations, he did not want to have it. "I didn't want to have an injection, so I pretended to have been immunized. I rolled up my shirt, held a cotton ball over my upper arm, and strolled past the immunization team as though I'd already had the shot."[6]

Soon afterward, he had to take care of two children with smallpox. "I took those children to quarantine. The young girl died. And then I got sick with smallpox and ended up in the same quarantine facility. I made myself miss the vaccine thinking I was cheating the others, but later it turned out I was cheating myself." Ali survived the speckled monster in 1977 and became the last person in the world who suffered naturally occurring smallpox.

Edward Jenner's work with smallpox opened a new era in medicine. His vaccine showed that diseases were not something people had to endure and hope for the best. His work provided hope for humanity because it showed that diseases could be fought and eventually defeated.

Jenner's work inspired many other great scientists who came after him. One of them was Louis Pasteur, who between 1880 and 1885 discovered a new method to create vaccines against chicken cholera, anthrax, and rabies. Pasteur proposed to use the term vaccine not only for smallpox immunization but also for any other similar method that would provide protection against a disease. Thanks to the groundbreaking work of Edward Jenner, vaccines today prevent many diseases and have significantly improved people's quality of life.

Challenges Ahead

The next global challenge is to eradicate another serious disease called polio. The polio virus lives in nerve tissue and destroys it, causing a child who is infected with it to become paralyzed. In 2002 one of the most active health

Edward Jenner: Conqueror of Smallpox

In 1977, Ali Maow Maalin of Somalia (above) was the last person on the planet to suffer from natural smallpox.

workers working on the polio campaign was Ali Maow Maalin, the same man who had the case of natural smallpox. Ali was forty-six years old, and the scars on his face had faded. But he had not forgotten his smallpox experience.

He knows how children dislike injections, so he tells them his story about what happened to him for avoiding a smallpox shot. "Because I had the sad experience of defying the vaccine and then suffered as a result, I now work as a polio vaccine agent with W.H.O." He travels around Marka explaining the need to vaccinate every child under five years of age. He knows vaccination saves lives and he is committed to help Somalia eradicate polio as soon as possible. "Somalia was the last country to have smallpox. I don't want it to be the last with polio."[7]

Activities

How Do Vaccines Work?

A vaccine teaches the body to build a defense against a disease. The body naturally makes such defenses each time it fights the germs that cause an infection. The fighting is done by the immune system, which is an army of cells and molecules that work together to kill invading germs.

While the immune system is working against the infection some special immune cells are being trained to quickly recognize and destroy the germ that caused the infection. If the person recovers, the immune system keeps its best fighting cells ready to find and destroy the germs as soon as they appear. If the same kind of germs infect that person again, the army of immune cells and molecules can destroy the germs so quickly that the person may not even feel sick. The person has "immunity" to the disease.

Jenner realized that a cowpox infection gives immunity to smallpox. Cowpox trains the immune system to attack the cowpox virus—and other viruses like it, such as the smallpox virus.

Vaccines Today

Since Jenner's time scientists have improved the way they prepare vaccines. Today vaccines are made in special laboratories. Each vaccine contains germs for a particular disease that have been weakened or killed. These germs train the immune system to attack them, but without causing the infection. Usually a nurse injects the vaccine into an arm or leg. Most people don't even feel sick after taking the shot, and they are protected against a dangerous disease.

But how can a doctor know a vaccinated person is really protected? The only way Jenner could check if cowpox had conferred immunity against smallpox was to infect the vaccinated person with smallpox germs. If the person did not get smallpox, then Jenner knew that the vaccination had worked. But if the vaccinated

111

person got smallpox, then Jenner would know the vaccine had not worked. This was a risky procedure because it put the person's life in danger if the vaccine had not worked.

Today doctors do not have to risk a person's health to check for immunity. Doctors perform blood laboratory tests instead. One of the first tests used was called immunoprecipitation. The test measures if a person's blood contains special molecules called antibodies to fight the germs the person was vaccinated against.

Before receiving a vaccine, a person's serum (the liquid part of the blood) normally does not precipitate, or bind to the germs that cause the disease. However, usually after vaccination antibodies appear in the blood. Antibodies bind to and neutralize the germs that cause that particular disease. This neutralization can be observed in a laboratory test called immunoprecipitation. It appears in the form of a precipitate, or a white dust coming out of the mixture of the immune serum and the germs bound together.

Immunity Test

The following experiment simulates an immunoprecipitation test. The simulation test compares the "serum" from a person not vaccinated with the serum of the same person a few weeks after vaccination.

Warning: handle epsom salts and ammonia carefully. Wash your hands after finishing your experiment, and discard all materials in the trash and the chemicals in the sink. Ask an adult to help you with this experiment.

Materials needed:

- Plastic or glass measuring cup
- Water
- Two small (4 oz) baby food jars, labeled BEFORE and AFTER
- Plastic measuring spoons
- 1 teaspoon of Epsom salts (magnesium sulfate)
- Spoon to stir
- 2 teaspoons of household ammonia

(ammonium hydroxide, household cleaner)

- Black paper

Procedure:

❶ Measure ¼ cup of water, which represents the blood serum of a person who has not been vaccinated. Divide it equally between both jars.

❷ Add 1 teaspoon of Epsom salts, which represents the vaccine substance, to the water in the jar labeled AFTER. Stir with the spoon until it dissolves completely, forming a clear solution.

❸ Using a clean spoon, add 2 teaspoons of ammonia, which represents the immunoprecipitation test, into each jar. DO NOT STIR.

Let both jars stand undisturbed for about 5 minutes on top of a black piece of paper. Observe the jars.

Question:

Which one has a precipitate forming? If this were a real serum sample, has vaccination succeeded?

Look at the following table with the results of immunoprecipitation tests for four different people:

Table of Immunoprecipitation Results		
Patient	**Before**	**After**
A	No	Yes
B	No	No
C	No	Yes
D	Yes	Yes

❶ In which patients did vaccination succeed?

❷ In which one did it not succeed?

❸ Which patient was already immune before vaccination?

Chronology

1749—Born on May 17, to Stephen and Sarah Jenner, in Berkeley, England.

1754—Deaths of parents.

1757—Enters Wotton-under-Edge grammar school and is inoculated.

1761—Becomes apprentice to Mr. John Ludlow, a family doctor in Chipping Sudbury.

1770—Moves to London to continue his medical studies under Dr. John Hunter, prominent scientist and physician.

1771—Return of Captain Cook from his first expedition on board the ship *Endeavor*.

1772—Returns to Berkeley and begins his country doctor's practice.

1775—Studies hibernating hedgehogs.

1778—Studies the blockage of coronary arteries in angina pectoris.

1784—Launches a hydrogen balloon.

1787—Buys The Chantry, his house at Berkeley, where he lived with his wife and children; studies the peculiar habits of the cuckoo bird.

1788—March 6: Marries Catherine Kingscote; founds the Gloucester Medical Society.

1789—Is elected as a Fellow of the Royal Society for his studies on the habits of the cuckoo bird; first son, Edward Jr., is born.

1792—Receives a diploma in medicine from the University of St. Andrews, Scotland.

1793—Death of John Hunter from a heart attack as a result of his angina pectoris.

1794—Birth of the Jenners' second child, Catherine.

1794–1795—Suffers a near-fatal attack of typhoid.

1796—May 14: Performs the first safe vaccination against smallpox on eight-year-old James Phipps from the cowpox pustule on the hand of Sarah Nelmes.

1797—Birth of the Jenners' third child, Robert.

1798—Pursues his studies on cowpox and smallpox; publishes his studies in "The Inquiry"; first vaccination in London, performed by Henry Cline.

1799—Jenner's vaccine begins to be distributed all over the world; publishes his second book on cowpox and smallpox, "Further Observations."

1800—Jenner's vaccine spreads to most European countries; July: First vaccination in Boston, Massachusetts.

1802—Receives the first grant from the king of ten thousand pounds.

1803—Formation of the Royal Jennerian Society for the Extermination of Smallpox in London; departure of the Spanish expedition carrying the vaccine to South and Central America and the Philippines.

1806—Receives second grant from the king, this time twenty thousand pounds.

1813—Receives the honorary title of Doctor in Medicine from the University of Oxford.

1815—September 13: Wife Catherine dies.

1823—January 26: Edward Jenner dies.

1967—The World Health Organization (WHO) in Geneva begins the worldwide campaign for the eradication of smallpox.

1977—Last recorded case of natural smallpox: Ali Maow Maalin in Somalia, Africa.

1980—May 8: Official ceremony of the declaration of global eradication of smallpox.

Chapter Notes

Chapter 1. "A Terrifying Experience"

1. John Baron, *The Life of Edward Jenner,*: With illustrations of his doctrines, and selections from his correspondence. (London: Henry Colburn, 1827), p. 14.

2. Ibid, p. 16.

3. Abbas M. Behbehani, *The Smallpox Story: In Words and Pictures* (Kansas City: University of Kansas Medical Center, 1988), p. 3.

4. Ibid, p. 1.

5. Herve Bazin, *The Eradication of Smallpox: Edward Jenner and the First and Only Eradication of a Human Infectious Disease*, trans. Andrew Morgan and Glenise Morgan (London: Academic Press, 2000), p. 5.

6. Ibid, p. 8.

7. Baron, p. 60.

Chapter 2. Rough Beginnings

1. Dorothy Mary Fisk, *Dr. Jenner of Berkeley* (London: Heineman, 1959), p. 3.

2. Ibid., p. 2.

3. Ibid., p. 16.

Chapter 3. Going to London

1. Dorothy Mary Fisk, *Dr. Jenner of Berkeley* (London: W. Heineman, 1959), p. 22.

2. Richard B. Fisher, *Edward Jenner 1749–1823*, (London: Andre Deutsch, Ltd. 1991), p. 22.

3. John Baron, *The Life of Edward Jenner* (London: Colburn, 1838), p. 25.

4. R. B. Fisher, p. 22.

5. Ibid., p. 25.
6. Ibid., p. 27.

Chapter 4. Sleeping Hedgehogs and Burning Candles

1. R. B. Fisher, *Edward Jenner 1749–1823* (London: Andre Deutsch, 1991), p. 32.

2. Herve Bazin, *The Eradication of Smallpox: Edward Jenner and the First and Only Eradication of a Human Infectious Disease*, trans. Andrew Morgan and Glenise Morgan (London: Academic Press, 2000), p. 24.

3. A. M. Behbehani, *The Smallpox Story: In Words and Pictures* (Kansas City: University of Kansas Medical Center, 1988), p. 42.

Chapter 5. On Bony Canals and Hydrogen Balloons

1. R. B. Fisher, *Edward Jenner 1749–1823* (London: Andre Deutsch, 1991), p. 53.

2. Ibid., p. 53.

3. Genevieve Miller, ed., *Letters of Edward Jenner and Other Documents Concerning the Early History of Vaccination*, (Baltimore: John Hopkins University Press, 1983), p. 3.

4. H. Bazin, *The Eradication of Smallpox: Edward Jenner and the First and Only Eradication of a Human Infectious Disease*, trans. A. Morgan and G. Morgan (London: Academic Press, 2000), p. 26.

Chapter 6. Of the Blizzard and Cuckoo Birds

1. D. Fisk, *Dr. Jenner of Berkeley* (London: W. Heineman, 1959), p. 84.

2. R. B. Fisher, *Edward Jenner 1749–1823* (London: Andre Deutsch, 1991), p. 29.

3. Edward Jenner, "Observations on the Natural History of the Cuckoo," *Philosophical Transactions of the Royal Society, London*, vol. 78, 1788, p. 219.

4. Ibid., p. 221.
5. R. B. Fisher, p. 50.
6. Ibid., p. 29.

Chapter 7. The Milkmaid's Fortune Is Her Face

1. Edward Jenner, *The Origin of Vaccine Inoculation* (London: S. Low, 1801).

2. Edward Jenner, *The Inquiry*, (London: S. Low, 1798).

3. H. Bazin, *The Eradication of Smallpox: Edward Jenner and the First and Only Eradication of a Human Infectious Disease*, trans. Andrew Morgan and Glenise Morgan (London: Academic Press, 2000), p. 36.

4. D. Fisk, Dr. Jenner of Berkeley (London: W. Heineman, 1959), p. 126.

Chapter 8. James Phipps

1. Edward Jenner, *Further Observations on the Variola Vaccinae, or Cow-Pox* (London: 1799), p. 14.

2. Edward Jenner, *Records of an Old Medical Society: Some Unpublished Manuscripts of Edward Jenner* (British Medical Journal, 1896), p. 1298.

3. Edward Jenner, *Further Observations*, p. 21.

4. R. B. Fisher, *Edward Jenner 1749–1823* (London: Andre Deutsch, 1991), p. 61.

5. Herve Bazin, *The Eradication of Smallpox: Edward Jenner and the First and Only Eradication of a Human Infectious Disease*, trans. Andrew Morgan and Glenise Morgan (London: Academic Press, 2000), p. 32.

6. Ibid., p. 38.

7. Edward Jenner, *The Inquiry* (London: S. Low, 1798), p. 27.

8. Ibid.

9. R. B. Fisher, p. 67.

Chapter 9. *The Inquiry*

1. E. Jenner, *Records of an Old Medical Society: Some Unpublished Manuscripts of Edward Jenner* (British Medical Journal, 1896), p. 1298.

2. H. Bazin, *The Eradication of Smallpox: Edward Jenner and the First and Only Eradication of a Human Infectious Disease*,

trans. Andrew Morgan and Glenise Morgan (London: Academic Press, 2000), p. 39.

    3. E. Jenner, *The Inquiry* (London: S. Low, 1798), p. 30.

    4. H. Bazin, p. 40.

Chapter 10. Conquering Smallpox

    1. H. Bazin, *The Eradication of Smallpox: Edward Jenner and the First and Only Eradication of a Human Infectious Disease*, trans. Andrew Morgan and Glenise Morgan (London: Academic Press, 2000), p. 40.

    2. Ibid., p. 71.

    3. Ibid., p. 74.

    4. R. B. Fisher, *Edward Jenner 1749–1823* (London: Andre Deutsch, 1991), p. 99.

    5. H. Bazin, p. 78.

    6. "Moon Nomenclature: Craters," *U.S. Geological Survey, Astrogeology Research Program*, n.d., <http://planetary names.wr.usgs.gov/moon/mooncrat.html> (March 11, 2005).

Chapter 11. The Last Case of Smallpox

    1. S. M. Wilson, "On the Matter of Smallpox," *Natural History*, vol. 103, no. 9, 1994, p. 64.

    2. Genevieve Miller, ed., *Letters of Edward Jenner and Other Documents Concerning the Early History of Vaccination* (Baltimore: John Hopkins University Press, 1983), p. 31.

    3. World Health Organization, *The Global Eradication of Smallpox: Final Report of the Global Commission for the Certification of Small Eradication, Geneva 1979*, (Geneva: World Health Organization, 1988), p. 40.

    4. Frank Fenner et al., *Smallpox and Its Eradication*, (Geneva: World Health Organization, 1988), <http://www.who.int/emc/diseases/smallpox/Smallpoxeradication.html (March 11, 2005).

    5. Ibid.

    6. World Health Organization, *Global Polio Eradication Initiative, Progress 2002* (Geneva: World Health Organization, 2002), p. 28.

    7. Ibid, p. 29.

Glossary

angina pectoris—Severe pain in the chest associated with an insufficient supply of blood to the heart.

apprentice—One who is learning a trade or occupation.

arm-to-arm transfer—Procedure of passing cowpox or smallpox matter from one person to another.

cowpox—A mild, contagious skin disease of cattle, usually affecting the udder, that is caused by a virus.

dissection—Separation or division of organs or tissues for the purpose of critical examination.

epidemic—The rapid and extensive spread of a disease by infection, which affects many individuals in an area or a population at the same time.

grant—A giving of funds or money for a specific purpose.

grease—A disease of horses that affects their hooves.

hedgehog—Any of several small insectivorous mammals of Europe, Africa, and Asia having the back covered with dense erectile spines and characteristically rolling into a ball for protection.

hibernation—An inactive or dormant state.

immune system—Group of specialized cells and molecules in the body that neutralize and destroy germs that cause diseases.

immunity—Resistance to infection by a specific germ.

inoculation—In Jenner's time the infection of a healthy person with a mild case of smallpox.

inquiry—A close examination of a matter in search for information or truth.

lancet—A surgical knife with a short, wide, pointed double-edged blade, used especially for making punctures and small incisions or cuts.

pus—A generally viscous, yellowish white fluid formed in infected tissue, consisting of white blood cells, dead cells, and germs.

pustule—A small, swollen elevation of the skin that is filled with pus.

quarantine—A period of time during which a person or material suspected of carrying a contagious disease is isolated to prevent the disease from spreading.

smallpox—A highly infectious, often fatal disease caused by a virus and characterized by high fever and aches with subsequent widespread eruption of pimples that blister, produce pus, and result in pockmarks. Also called variola.

speckled—Covered with speckles.

spurious—Not genuine; false.

susceptible—Easily affected.

vaccination—Administration of a vaccine in order to protect against a particular disease.

vaccine—A preparation containing a disease germ that has been weakened or killed so that it stimulates the immune system to fight against the germ but is incapable of causing severe infection. In Jenner's time a preparation from the cowpox virus that protects against smallpox.

variola—See smallpox.

virus—Any of various simple submicroscopic particles that often cause disease.

Further Reading

Books

Christopher, J. and B. Jones. *Riding the Jetstream: The Story of Ballooning from Montgolfier to Breitling*. London: John Murray Publishers, 2002.

Collier, James Lincoln. *Vaccines*. New York: Benchmark Books, 2004.

Hopkins, Donald R. *The Greatest Killer: Smallpox in History*. Illinois: The University of Chicago Press, 2002.

Marrin, Albert. *Dr. Jenner and the Speckled Monster: The Search for the Smallpox Vaccine*. New York: Dutton Children's Books, 2003.

Internet Addresses

MicrobeWorld
<www.microbeworld.org>

MicrobeWorld explores the world of microbes with vivid images and descriptions. Learn about microbiology, what microbiologists do, and much more.

The Jenner Museum
<http://www.jennermuseum.com>

Viruses
<http://www.microbeworld.org/microbes/virus/default.aspx>

What Is Smallpox?
<http://www.kidshealth.org/kid/health_problems/infection/smallpox.html>

Index